FRAGMENTS

Maura Pierlot

fragmentstheplay.com

Big Ideas PRESS

PRESS

FRAGMENTS © MAURA PIERLOT 2019

BIG IDEAS PRESS

First published in paperback edition in 2021 by Big Ideas Press, an independent press based in Canberra. The e-book of this playscript was published in 2020 by Australian Plays (now Australian Plays Transform) and can be purchased directly from their website: https://apt.org.au.

A catalogue record for this work is available from the National Library of Australia

ISBN: 978-0-6450998-0-5 (pbk)

Cover design and typesetting: Monique-Mai Designs
Cover photo: Novel Photographic

To everyone who is struggling and searching to connect.

SCRIPT

CONTENTS

Monologues/Scenes

A Study Guide including curriculum links and classroom activities
is included at the back of this book.

About the Playwright

Maura Pierlot is an award-winning author and playwright who hails from New York but has called Canberra home since 1991. Her writing delves into complex issues including memory, identity, self and, more recently, mental health.

Photo: Novel Photographic

Maura's professional theatrical debut, *Fragments*, enjoyed a sellout season at The Street Theatre in October 2019, programmed for ACT Mental Health Month. Maura has won the Hothouse Theatre's SOLO Monologue Competition for her play *Tapping Out*, which went on to receive three awards at Short+Sweet Sydney (2017). A former medical news reporter and editor of *Australian Medicine*, Maura also writes for children and young adults. In 2017 she was named winner of the CBCA Aspiring Writers Mentorship Program, and recipient of the Charlotte Waring Barton Award, for her young adult manuscript, *Freefalling* (now *True North*). Maura's first picture book, *The Trouble in Tune Town*, launched in May 2018 at the National Library of Australia, won the 2018 ACT Writing and Publishing Award (Children's category), along with international accolades.

Maura has a bachelor's degree, master's degree and doctorate, each in philosophy, specialising in ethics. When she's not busy creating, she visits schools and libraries as a guest reader and speaker, serves as a Role Model for Books in Homes, and contributes reviews for the Children's Book Council of Australia's online magazine, *Reading Time*.

From the Writer

Rarely presenting as neat packages, mental health issues often involve feelings and behaviours with jagged edges and blurred origins. *Fragments* embodies the theme that stress at home, at school and in life is challenging young people beyond their usual coping abilities, leaving them disenfranchised and vulnerable.

I wrote *Fragments* to start a conversation, to give a sense of agency to young people while reaching out to their peers, families and the community. It's only when we speak openly about mental health issues – without fear or judgment – that we can chip away at the stigma that prevents many people from seeking help. This is especially important for young people. So much of adolescent life is spent looking inwards that it's perhaps not surprising that mental health issues are often internalised and ignored.

Following the play's sell-out season in Canberra in late 2019, the city was besieged by smoke in a summer like no other. Then, on the heels of the devastating bushfires that heralded 2020, COVID-19 crashed into our collective consciousness. Lockdown, social distancing and hand sanitising were the new normal as people all over the world became disconnected, isolated and fearful. Mental health issues (especially anxiety), already at an all-time high, skyrocketed.

In bringing *Fragments* to the public, I wanted to explore the healing that may come from looking outwards – from our connectedness to others and our realisation that we are not alone. The eight monologues presented here are pieces – *fragments* – of the countless stories to be told. It is my hope that this work finds its way into schools and communities across Australia and overseas, that it sparks meaningful dialogue, and that we can open our hearts and minds to recognise ourselves in each other.

Maura Pierlot

FRAGMENTS

By Maura Pierlot

Supported by

Logline

Raw and real. Follow eight teens as they struggle to find hope and their sense of self in the face of adversity.

Summary

I feel like I'm a piece, a fragment that's missing all the good bits, but I don't know where to find the rest … the parts I need to work properly. I bet they wouldn't fit anyway.

Eight young people navigating high school and beyond, each struggling to hold on – to family, to friends, to a piece of themselves. Perhaps you know them. The bubbly girl who keeps telling you she's okay. The high achiever who's suddenly so intense. The young teen obsessed with social media. The boy challenged by communication. Every single day they, and others, are working hard to keep it together. So hard, they don't see their friends are struggling, too.

Speaking to the complexity, uncertainty and challenges of our lives today, *Fragments* is an honest and unflinching work, and a must-read for young people and adults alike.

Provenance of Fragments

Fragments enjoyed a sellout season at The Street Theatre, Canberra (23 - 27 October 2019). The debut production, directed by Shelly Higgs, was supported by the ACT Government (through artsACT), LJ Hooker Canberra City and the Mental Health Community Coalition ACT.

An earlier version of the *Fragments* monologues was performed at Pioneer Theatre, 14 - 17 November 2018, directed by James Hartley, Upper Crass Theatre Company. Selected monologues have been performed at various theatre festivals in Australia and overseas.

This work has been developed with support from MPS Travel+Tours Award, Capital Arts Patrons' Organisation; Ainslie+Gorman Arts Centres, Ralph Indie Program; Australian Cultural Fund; Bundanon Trust; and The Street Theatre's First Seen Program. Dramaturgy by Shelly Higgs, Caroline Stacey, James Hartley and Gin Savage with input from Suzanne Ingelbrecht, Rochelle Whyte and Adelaide Rief.

From the Director

Fragments is an incredibly important work for our times, connecting us to stories of the here and now and giving voice to those who are not always able to speak up. Not only does the work tackle a myriad of issues faced by adolescents, it speaks to these challenges in a way that young people will understand and relate to. How Maura got into the character's heads so accurately is testament to her talent as a writer.

It was important that the production's next gen actors felt comfortable sharing their own experiences and inevitably brought some parts of themselves to the roles. It was surprising how many personal stories were shared in the rehearsal room and I would encourage anyone approaching this text to do so knowingly; it's a vehicle not only for the characters' expression, but often the actors' own. Being a series of solo pieces, *Fragments* offers wide scope and application for this text. The stories stand alone and can be performed separately or even a handful at a time. What is important is how they give voice.

The challenge we faced presenting the pieces together as a whole was to create cohesion to the journey. The play is hopeful, yes, but it's also careful not to minimise. Ultimately, we found our way by realising this play is one from disconnection through to connection. By the end of *Fragments* there is a sense that these characters have finally heard and seen each other, but more than that, that the audience may have lowered the walls between themselves for a moment and really seen each other, too. *Fragments* so desperately seeks "oneness". And looking around at the audience on closing night, a room full of people talking, sharing their own stories and connecting, a meeting of humanity through mutual experience ... I think it's fair to say that this text holds that power.

Shelly Higgs

ABOUT THE PRODUCTION

Produced by The Street, *Fragments* premiered at The Street Theatre, Canberra, 23 - 27 October 2019, programmed for Mental Health Month, with the following cast:

WILL	Tom Bryson
FREYA	Marni Mount
VIJAY	Prithvi Saxena
REENA	Erin Pierlot
MILA	Linda Chen
NICKY	Damon Baudin
LEXY	Holly Johnson
MASON	Zane Menegazzo

Director, Shelly Higgs

Artistic Director/CEO, The Street Theatre, Caroline Stacey

Stage and Costume Designer, Imogen Keen

Lighting Designer, James Tighe

Sound Designer, Kyle Sheedy

Cultural Consultant, Daniel Berthon

The production enjoyed a sell-out season and recevied critical acclaim.

An earlier version of *Fragments* (monologues only) was performed at Pioneer Theatre in Castle Hill, NSW, 14 - 17 November 2018, directed by James Hartley, Upper Crass Theatre Company.

With funding from artsACT, the playwright is creating a new work, based on *Fragments*, for the digital space.

ABOUT THE STREET

The Street Theatre is Canberra's leading creative producer and theatre company dedicated to ambitious contemporary live performance, as well as presenting artistically bold performances from other places. The Street's innovative use of set, sound and lighting created a visceral sense of the mental health themes of the work and the technological world in which the characters live.

CHARACTERS

WILL,   16 (M)

FREYA,   15 (F)

VIJAY,   14 (M)

REENA,   13 (F)

MILA,   18 (F)

NICKY,   17 (trans F presenting as M)

LEXY,   17 (F)

MASON,   18 (M)

SETTING

The action of *Fragments* takes place in the minds and hearts of an ordinary group of eight young people. Although set in Australia, their stories could take place anywhere.

PRODUCTION NOTES

We encourage anyone producing or casting this work to consider performers and production personnel from diverse backgrounds.

MONOLOGUE SYNOPSES

Short Circuit

Drawn to rhythm, Will struggles in a world of words, unable to connect to the girl of his dreams, but refusing medication that will make him think like everyone else.

In My Head

On the outside Freya's a normal teen, but on the inside, she's fighting anxiety every single day, alone and unable to tell anyone that she needs help.

Good for Nothing

Worried he'll never be tall enough, handsome enough or smart enough, Vijay turns to social media to chat up girls at school, with devastating consequences.

Picture Perfect

Convinced she's fat, Reena relies on filters to market a better version of herself online, revelling in praise from a growing legion of followers.

Pretty Stupid

Reeling from an abrupt reality check, a young woman sues her school and family for failing to prepare her for life after graduation.

She

Every day she fights to be heard, to dress as she wants, to be who she is ... until one day when she must make a choice, knowing she can never be free as long as he lives.

Roller Coaster

Lexy is determined to internalise her family struggles until a chance meeting opens the floodgates and changes the course of her life.

Now You See Me

Everyone's so busy looking up to school captain, Mason that they don't recognise the debilitating depression that is taking over his life.

FIGHT SONG (In My Skin)

Eight young people on the edge, helpless, hopeless. Their voice is unified, yet they are unaware of each other's presence.

                    REENA
In my skin.

                    NICKY
I'm here.

                    FREYA
Fighting.

                    WILL
Still fighting.

                    MILA
Feeding off the scraps.

                    VIJAY
You toss out.

                    LEXY
With the trash.

                    MASON
All of you.

                    NICKY
The ones who call me names.

MILA
The ones who ignore me.

VIJAY
At school.

LEXY
At home.

REENA
Everywhere.

FREYA
I don't need you.

WILL
I don't need anyone.

MASON:
I don't know what I need.

Cast circles around MASON as soundscape moves to ominous tone. It is not clear whether the chorus is encouraging MASON to keep fighting or to give up.

ALL
Keep going.

MASON
I'm so tired of fighting.

ALL
One step, then another.

                    MASON
        I can't do this anymore.

                     ALL
        Stop!

                    MASON *(Disoriented)*
        Where am I?

*Audio becomes layered, distorted as the
cast moves en masse, a dark cloud smothering
MASON.*

Lights/music out.

TRUTH AND LIES (Stranded)

Lights up. The group fragments into their characters. Upbeat.

REENA
Everyone wants to be me.

VIJAY
I get girls.

WILL
I want to be normal.

FREYA
I'm fine, really.

LEXY
I can look after myself.

NICKY
I know exactly who I am.

MILA
I've got the world at my feet.

MASON
It's all good. Seriously.

Metaphysical shift.

REENA
I'm flawed.

                    VIJAY
I'm boring.

                     WILL
I'm broken.

                    FREYA
I'm afraid.

                     LEXY
I'm confused.

                    NICKY
I'm torn.

                     MILA
I'm worthless.

                    MASON
I'm lost.

                      ALL
I'm stranded.

SHORT CIRCUIT

Will taps a quick rhythm, stopping suddenly.

> There's a short circuit. In my head. Sixteen years of malfunction, thanks to faulty wires … a supercharged current overloading a path of low resistance, exceeding capacity. It's burning out the fuses, tripping the breakers.

Pause.

> I've never been good with words. I prefer to tap.

Taps, soon settling into a comfortable rhythm.

> It's simple ... predictable. Not all taps are made equal, you know. No, no, NO. They're jam packed with meaning.

Taps: Da DA da da DA da da DA DA.

> Note the syncopation, how the emphasis is on the downbeat. That means, 'Hurry up, I'm excited'.

Changes to a slower, monotone tap.

That's the 'I've just bored myself
into a heart attack' tap … often

featured in Maths class. Hang on,
here's the best one!

Two quick taps.

I give up. No, that's what the tap
means! It's what wrestlers do when
they've had enough. They don't shout
'Help!' or 'I surrender'. No way!

Tapping twice.

They tap out. And the match is over.
Simple.

Beat.

Sometimes I feel like tapping out.
Calm down! I'm not talking 'bout
that! I'm just saying, tapping gives
me something to focus on. Something
meaningful.

You know those really sad movies,
where the kid's dog dies, and you
sit there all misty-eyed, thinking,
I don't even cry. Where's this shit
coming from? Or someone trips when
they're walking and you crack up,
even though a little voice in your
head says, Hope they didn't hurt
themselves. It's instinct. Your body

doing something without your head
telling it to.

Heartbeat is heard.

Listen, do you hear that? You gotta
pay attention! It's soft, just a
murmur really. Whenever I think of
Freya, it's there. The rhythm. It's
strong and steady with reverb.

Fights unseen opponent with good physicality.

A techno beat revving my heart …
that skips and holds, cutting in
when I least expect it, flipping time
signatures left and right, breaking
all the rules.

Last night at the party, I watched
Freya from across the room. Twirling
her hair around her finger, eyes
wide open, taking in everyone
and everything around her. And I
thought, this is it! This is the
night I'm gonna finally tell her
how I feel! It took forever to take
those steps, and when I finally
rocked up and looked in her eyes,
all I could think was, 'You're
my hub. You're my connection.'
But I couldn't get the words out.
The thoughts were in my head but
the formations were too fast, too
random. Freya smiled, leaning in

like she couldn't hear me. Her hand
brushed my arm and I could feel my
pores opening up to breathe in all
her energy. Then whoa, key change,
minor to major transposed, gnawing
my insides, tightening, tightening
all the frazzled wires in my head,
till the sweetest riff tuned in and
the sound was crisp and clear, the
pitch perfect. My mouth opened to
make a made a sound I've never heard
before.

With feeling.

I love you. But the progression was
too abrupt, no time to modulate, and
before I could suck back the words,
they had already rushed in her ears,
feroce, and she gagged them up, short
and sharp… staccato. Something about
friends.

I don't talk like other people.
I don't think like other people.
Dad's always telling me, 'It's good
to be different'. So why's school
trying to make us all the same?
Friendly, sporty, smart. Like Mason,
poster boy for school captain. You
know, doctors do it too … use big
words, like something has to be
named to be understood. Labels that
put people in boxes, as though our
'differentness' is all the same, so

all the 'normal' people can feel
comfortable in their discomfort,
so they can understand, so YOU can
understand, something that can't
possibly be understood unless it's
in your head, unless you're living
it every single moment of every day.
You say I'm on the spectrum, that
I'm different but different to who?
You? Spectrum's a bullshit word.
It's a rainbow with no start or
finish, something that makes you feel
good but when you reach out to touch
it, nothing's there.

I don't want any meds! I don't
wanna 'even out' my mood. I don't
wanna patch job, I need to 'increase
capacity' to prevent overload. It's
simple engineering. No meds are
gonna show me how connect … how to
find the right words to express how I
feel. They didn't work for Dad. When
he left, there were so many words
flying between him and Mum, diving
and swooping, attacking, then none
for a long time.

Long pause.

Language is tricky. It's meant to
bring people together but I reckon
it does the opposite. Cos the words
don't have meaning, it's the emotion
that comes behind them. The chords

that make you weep, when caressed
on a violin, but get your toes
tapping when strummed on a banjo.

Beat.

I reckon I can work things out on my
own.

Starts tapping.

If I can find the rhythm. I just need
to learn the beats and stresses,
the run-ons and pauses, so I know
the words and patterns that make
sense. The ones that produce a sound
so pure when they come together in
harmony.

* * * * *

IN MY HEAD

A nervous Freya takes her place on stage,
as if giving a speech. She flashes an awkward
smile before speaking.

>Hi, I'm Freya. I'm fifteen and in
>Year 10. That's right, two more
>years to go!
>
>I play guitar and netball, and I
>have the greatest friends! What do I
>wanna be? Well, I'm leaning towards
>law but commerce is my backup.

Giggly.

>Who knows? Maybe I'll do both!

Smile/energy slowly disappear.

>That's me at school. Smiling like
>I've got everything under control.
>But I don't. Problem is everyone
>thinks you have to be bleeding or
>bandaged to be in pain, like if they
>can't see the damage it's not real.
>If you could see inside my head,
>you'd know it's real. It's tsunamis,
>terrorism, global warming, war,
>bushfires, nuclear attacks, drink
>spiking, date rape, serial killers,
>cyclones.

You think it's funny like none of
this stuff is gonna happen dontcha?
But it could happen, you can't
guarantee that it won't! And when
my head's not flipping me out about
shit far away, it's choking me with
stuff closer to home: my grades, my
future, why my friends are bitching
about me. No one understands me.
How can they, when I don't even
understand me?

Energetically.

You wanna know what anxiety feels
like? It feels like all the cells
in my body are colliding, like I'm
running an obstacle course that
never ends and my heart can't keep
up. Anxiety is every nerve in my
body on fire, acid coursing through
my veins … all the hair on my head
bursting through the follicles, each
strand pushing with all its might,
desperate to break through, to not
be smothered.

Breathy.

Anxiety is when I gulp and swallow
but there's no air cos my lungs are
crushed by fear, knowing it's around
every corner, waiting, waiting, and
the second I let my guard down,
all the thoughts crammed in my head

explode and I can't feel anything …
except the sting of my fingernails
gouging my skin, telling me I'm
still here.

Pause.

Fight or flight doesn't make any
sense cos in the moment you can't
do either. So I do the only thing
I can. I cover my head and I don't
even care if I suffocate cos I'm
suffocating every single day. Then
I scream away all the bad thoughts
— a roar so deafening it shakes the
walls, but no one hears me. No one
ever hears me.

I know it's normal to feel a bit
anxious now and again. But is it
normal to see only the bad things
in the world? To magnify everything
till it's so blurry I can't even
remember what I'm afraid of?
Anxiety's tricky cos most of the
time I look just like everyone else.
And if I tell anyone what's inside
my head, that I'm dying inside, that
I can't breathe, they say … 'Freya,
can you just be happy for once?'
Or they laugh, like I'm some drama
queen, and walk away. And that's
even worse. So I put on my mask to
make everyone comfortable. Happiness
is contagious, cos if I'm smiling on

the outside, everything's gotta be
okay on the inside, right?

I watched the daily parade at lunch
today. Mason coming up the path,
beaming, everyone following him
like he's Jesus. Another day in the
life of school captain. He turned
to me and smiled as he walked past,
and I wondered if he was wearing a
mask too. Then the bell rang. Mr
del Vecchio came out of nowhere and
asked me, 'Are you okay?' My ears
heard him alright, but I couldn't
take my eyes off this long wiry hair
poking out from his baseball cap and
...

Motioning to corner of mouth.

The little smidge of tomato sauce he
had right here. I screamed inside,
trying to get my head and heart
and every muscle in my body to work
together, to find the words to tell
him no, I wasn't okay, I wasn't okay
at all. I opened my mouth but my
jaw clenched, trapping the words at
the back of my throat. And when they
finally escaped, they didn't sound
like my words at all. 'I'm fine.
Really.'

No one can understand what's in my
head. Except maybe this one girl at

school… Riva or Reena, or something
like that. She's always plugged in,
posing, her music blasting so loud
that everyone knows her playlist.
Her smile's so big it can't be real.
Sometimes I wanna go up and check out
her mask. To see if she's tuning in
or tuning out. To see if she loves
the noise or if it's the silence
that scares her. Well, I'll take her
silence. I crave the stillness. No
triggers. No inputs. No possibility
of overload.

I wish I had a remote control … for
life. I'd rewind to a few years ago.
Before all the worries crept in my
head. I'd never fast forward, no
way! I'd just hit mute or pause. And
no more chatter.

Yeah, just mute and pause. That's
all I need.

* * * * *

CLASS DISMISSED (Don't)

Characters push back from each other.

MILA

Don't try to understand me.
I'm an enigma.

LEXY

Don't try to tame me.
I'm wild but never free.

NICKY

Don't try to fix me.
I'm not broken.

REENA

Don't try to praise me.
I'm not who you think.

FREYA

Don't try to comfort me.
Your words have no power.

MASON

Don't try to save me.
My wounds are too deep.

WILL

Don't try to complete me.
I'm missing a piece.

VIJAY
Don't try to know me.
There's nothing to see.

GOOD FOR NOTHING

Vijay scrolls through his social media feed.

I'm not good at rugby, or cricket.
Or basketball. Any sport really. I
love acting and singing. But I'm not
very good at those either. To fit in,
you gotta be good at something. My
brain ticks over, but not as fast
as it should for all the crap I'm
expected to learn at school. And
I'm not a 'people person'. I'm super
funny in my head but the humour
always gets lost on the way out.
I've got just enough testosterone to
not get beaten up all the time but
not enough to do anything with.

School's constantly pushing us to
'strive for excellence'. The problem
is the more you try, the more you
see the massive gap between what's
possible and what's real. It's like
eating healthy food and exercising
all the time, taking vitamins even,
and everyone's having a growth spurt
but you. Suddenly you realise you're
never gonna grow as much as you want
cos you're just not made that way.
Effort doesn't always equal reward.
Except maybe for Mason. He's smart,
sporty and seriously good-looking.
No, I'm not gay. Any tool can see

the guy's genetically blessed.
Only one more term till he and his
perfect genes graduate but there'll
be another Mason next year. There
always is. Just to remind me of
everything I'm not.

I'm just like everyone else at
school. We listen to the same music,
watch the same shows, crack up at
the same memes so how come I'm never
invited to the good parties? How
come no one wants to hang out with
me? I'm Aussie, born and bred but to
everyone else, I'm Vijay, the Indian
guy. I'm walking the tightrope
between East and West, trying to
fit in at school while respecting
my parents and tradition. Mum means
well but she's the queen of mixed
messages. She's forever telling me,
'Vijay, you're only in Year 9, it's
too early to think about girls.'
Then she'll mention how wonderful
it'd be, how … easy, if one day I
just happened to meet a girl from
Punjab. I didn't think arranged
marriages were legal in Australia
… except maybe on Married at First
Sight. Or she'll tell me there's
plenty of time to figure out what I'm
good but in her next breath, she's
saying …'V, you need study harder,
how are you going to make your
mark?' Make my mark? I'm fourteen.

I have other shit on my mind. Like,
why haven't I grown in two years?
When's my skin gonna clear up? Am
I ever gonna get abs… like Mason's?
He's so cool and detached, like he's
too good for this world … no wonder
all the girls are after him. But
what girl's gonna go for …

Holding up shirt to expose lack of abs.

This?

I don't even know how to talk to a
girl face to face. At school they
travel in groups, always whispering,
or rolling their eyes. It's so …
confusing. I've got my eyes this one
girl, Reena so I've started a new
training program, ya know, Snapchat,
to build some social media muscle.
A few days ago I finally worked up
the nerve and sent her a pic of my
obese cat stretched out on the sofa,
watching TV. Everyone knows girls
love animals! And sure enough, she
replied seconds later. A spider
on the wall, just above her fairy
lights. Half an hour of random pics
later, I started Snapchatting a few
other girls. In no time I had twenty
streaks going so I moved up to the
next level: Messenger! I started
with one word — Hey — and Reena sent
back the same with a smiley face.

The good one with the rosy cheeks. The great thing about emojis is they say so much in so little space. And everyone can understand them. It's the universal language. The other night she asked how I did on my English essay so I sent her a pile of poo and the scream emoji and she sent back a hahahahahahahaaha that went on for four lines. That's some serious laughter.

Whenever I'm texting, the words flow. I'm funny, understanding, wise. I'm not that Indian guy with the strange lunch, I'm every guy. I'm a helping hand, a sounding board, a shoulder to cry on. I know exactly what to say, how to get girls to relax and tell me their problems. They're always asking for advice about some drama with their friends. Girls get so worked up over stupidest things, and when I tell them the easy fix, they say I'm so wise and great to talk to. Listen to this!

Grabs phone and reads messages.

'You are amazing! Love heart, love heart.' And the love hearts are red, not some lame yellow or purple. That means it's legit. Reena and I were getting along so well online I figured it was time to meet up

outside of school so I asked her to
the movies. She replied straight
away with emojis … the rolling on
the floor with laughter ones. Twenty-
two of them. So, I messaged, What's
the matter? Did I do something
wrong? But she blocked me. Then all
her friends blocked me. When I went
up to her locker after school today,
she held up her Maths text as a
shield, like she was blocking me in
life too.

I'm such an idiot. How could I think
Reena liked me? How could I think
anyone'd like me? When I don't even
know who I am, or what I want to be.
When I'm just a guy who's good for
nothing.

* * * * *

PICTURE PERFECT

Reena stares in the mirror, prodding and pinching her body.

Fat! Fat! FAT!

Stands back for full view before addressing audience.

The only thing not fat is my head. Actually, it's too small for my body. Great, I'm deformed too.

At the portrait gallery I went to with Nan last week, there was a huge black and white photo of an old woman sitting at a café. Her cheeks were all wrinkly and droopy, like our pug Otis, and she was wearing the skimpiest outfit, just a singlet and drawstring shorts. It was kinda gross cos rolls of fat were escaping everywhere, like sausage meat popping out of the casing. But she had the biggest smile, like she was a beauty queen decked out in the most expensive designer gown ever. My brain was screaming, 'Look away' but my eyes weren't listening. I voted that one for People's Choice cos a great photo captures your attention, makes you react. Nan didn't vote. She said, 'Nasreena'

— cos she still can't call me Reena like everyone else — 'Nasreena, a great portrait captures a person's essence, so how can anyone judge another person's photo?' And I thought, 'Oh my God, I love that word!' Ehhh - ssssssence.

Studies herself in mirror.

I'm still trying to find my essence but I don't know what I'm searching for. Is it a sparkle? Does it change all the time? Will other people see it through this?

Grabs her flesh.

I wish I could be put through a photocopier. I'd hit sixty percent reduction and voila! Instant happiness! Cos except for that old lady in the pic, it's skinny girls who have the biggest smiles on their faces. And they're everywhere! Skinny girls in magazines with stick legs in high heels carrying oversized handbags. Skinny girls on TV in string bikinis frolicking in the surf, showing off their thigh gaps.

Scanning her feed.

They're online, too. I mean,
hello? Have you ever checked out
Instagram? The whole point is to
be seen, living and loving life. To
have people follow you. To wanna
be you. All my friends have over
a thousand followers and ya know
how many I have? Three hundred
ninety-six! Cos no one wants to
flick through photos of fatties! But
I've changed all that. Yep, you're
looking at 'NazzyXO' with … wait
for it … twelve hundred twenty-four
followers.

Checks phone, smiling.

Make that twelve hundred twenty-
eight followers.

How'd I do it? Well it's funny,
cos I used to hate getting my photo
taken … until I discovered these
awesome apps to create a better
version of me. Someone taller,
thinner, tanner. I can change
my hair, my clothes, even my eye
colour. I mean, there's no point
being on Facebook and Instagram if
you look like shit, right? But with
the right apps, anything's possible.
There's even a formula: Photo,
Filter, Caption. See, the trick is
making the photos look natural, like
you just happen to be out and …

Poses for selfies.

> Photo: My legs, beach in background.
> Filter: Cool Breeze. Caption: Summer
> days, sun emoji, thumbs up! Photo:
> My lips with a glimpse of my bra.
> Filter: Mayfair. Caption: Up close
> and personal, winky face. Photo:
> My butt, photoshopped. Obviously.
> Filter: Black and white … it's all
> about the vibe. Caption: Tongue out
> dollar emoji.

> So what if I'm only thirteen? It's
> not like anyone's gonna find out.
> No one even knows it's me! That's
> cos I use a filter for all my pics.
> Enough so they look like me, but
> not enough that they look like me,
> if ya know what I mean. So what if
> it's not really me? It's the future
> me, the one I aspire to. If you're
> looking for a dress, you don't buy
> the first one you try on, right? You
> go through a few and pick the one
> that's the best fit. That's what I'm
> doing. Shopping for the best version
> of me. Cos why would I wanna be me
> when I could be …

Holds up phone.

> Me! NazzyXO is perfect, and everyone
> loves her.

Checks phone, excited.

> Check out these comments: 'Killer,
> knife emoji, flame. Yum, tongue out
> emoji. Beauty.' See?
>
> Some 'social media expert' came to
> our school the other day to tell
> all us girls to love our bodies. But
> she would say that cos she was fat.
> And just like all the other boring
> speakers, her idea of helping was to
> scare us into not doing anything.
> She went on and on about too much
> screen time leading to mental health
> problems, all cos of FOMO, ya know,
> fear of missing out. I so wanted to
> put up my hand and say, 'Uh, how
> 'bout not being online leading to
> mental health problems?' Like the
> time I didn't have my phone for three
> days, cos the stupid phone shop took
> forever to fix my home button, and
> when I finally got it back, it was
> like, 'Hello, what planet am I on?
> Cos nothing I'm reading is making
> any sense.' If I could be on my phone
> twenty-four seven, everything'd be
> okay, except then this guy at school,
> Vijay, sees I'm online and keeps
> chatting me up, going for streaks.
> He started off nice, but now he's a
> bit weird. He's always sending these
> random pics of objects or messaging
> me, trying to keep the convo going

like no one ever taught him how to
say 'Bye'. I don't know what he's
thinking but whatever it is, I'm not
interested. I want the hot guy. I
just don't know how to get him. Yet.

Phone buzzes.

Oh my God! Ruck33's following me!
And I'm not surprised. NazzyXO has
the right essence. I'd wanna meet up
with her too!

Checks image on phone closely.

Ah, thirty-three, I bet it's Mason!
That's his rugby number. Half my
year has a crush on him. Yeah,
he's five years older but that won't
matter when he's 21 and I'm 16. I
know! I'll Snapchat him!

*Takes selfie and sends. Seconds later, phone
buzzes.*

Okay, guess it's NOT Mason… or maybe
it is! Maybe he has a second account
too!

Checks phone.

Hmm, it kinda looks like him but
it's hard to tell. All the pics are
just pieces: a close-up of an eye,
half a mouth, a knee … nice pecs!

She hesitates for a moment then takes another photo, this one more provocative, and sends. Phone buzzes instantly and she checks screen, excited.

And abs!

Phone buzzes again.

Oooh, he wants more pics! Guess he likes what he sees.

She unbuttons her blouse for racier photo. She hesitates, longer than before, then hits 'send'. Her phone buzzes seconds later. She recoils, clearly shocked by the image/message on screen, then shoves the phone in her pocket, checking her surrounds to make sure no one else has seen.

* * * * *

DISTORTION (Subtext)

Unless named, performers are not in character and serve as a chorus of approval.

ALL (TO MASON)
Your abs are amazing.

LEXY
He's got it so easy.

ALL (TO LEXY)
I love your hair.

WILL
That's her one good feature.

ALL (TO WILL)
Your brain is unreal.

FREYA
That's not good, ya know.

ALL (TO FREYA)
Your smile's contagious.

VIJAY
Too bad it's fake.

ALL (TO VIJAY)
You're so funny.

                    REENA
Looking.

                 ALL (TO REENA)
You're so good to talk to.

                    NICKY
By text.

                 ALL (TO NICKY)
You've got such a cool style
for a guy … or a girl.

                    MILA
What are you anyway?

                 ALL (TO MILA)
You're so beautiful…

                    MASON
She's so full of herself.

PRETTY STUPID

Mila approaches the audience confidently.

> Okay, so … I used to be the "It
> girl". Ya know, pretty, popular,
> smart, sporty. I'm not trying to
> brag but my face and body fit the
> golden ratio. That's right, like the
> Fibonacci numbers? And inner beauty,
> well, that comes hand in hand cos
> when you look good, you feel good. I
> mean, if you had a choice of looking
> at a work of art all day or a pile
> of rubbish, you'd go for the art,
> right? That's why all the girls at
> school were always hanging off me,
> like my popularity was contagious.
> They think I don't see through them,
> fawning over my every word.

Exaggerated tone.

> 'Oh Mila, you're soooo funny!'
> Except I'm not really. But that
> doesn't stop me from telling them
> some lame joke just to see their
> reaction. I still remember the first
> one I told them in Year 3. Where did
> Napoleon keep his armies?

Pause.

> In his sleevies! Well, they threw

their heads back and cackled.
Allegra couldn't catch her breath.
I thought she was having a heart
attack. That's when I realised
beauty is more than skin deep.
It's power.

I've always known I was pretty.
Beautiful, everyone says, but I'm
not stuck up enough to call myself
that. I think I sensed it growing
up. The looks, the attention.
The jealousy. How all my friends
copied me — my hair, my clothes,
my expressions. How the guys would
stare then make some dumb excuse
to come up and talk to me. How
the teachers would nod and smile
whenever I raised my hand in class.
So surprise, surprise, I was the
one who always got the awards, the
one whose photo was always in the
school magazine, the one who got the
lead in the play, the one who was
always asked to speak at assembly.
If school was a TV show, then I was
the star.

Problem is the show's been cancelled.
'Perspective, Mila', you're thinking,
right? 'You made it! You graduated!
Take a load off, enjoy your gap year
before starting the adventure called
life. What're you worrying your
pretty little head about?'

Well, I'll tell you what. First, I
got my ATAR. And despite studying
nonstop I didn't even crack ninety.
So much for being smart. Stupid
Allegra got 96 — how is that
even possible? 'Don't worry about
scaling, study what you love and
you'll do fine.' That's what all the
teachers told us. So even though
my grades were heaps better than
Allegra's, she scaled way up with
Law and Commerce. Why the hell I
did Drama I'll never know. And now,
thanks to my crap ATAR, I can't get
into any of the courses I want, and
there's no way I'm gonna live at
home. I can't live at home.

My mistake? I fell for the 'Big
Lie'. The one school fed us year
after year, that if we worked hard,
the rewards would follow. That if we
stepped up, we'd be noticed.

Leans in as if revealing a confidence.

Hey Mason, if you're listening, you
might want to give up already.

I stepped up better than anyone so
why can't I find a job? I've been
to every shop in the goddamn mall.
Half the shopkeepers wouldn't even
talk to me, the others said, 'Check
online' the second they spotted my

resume. One snooty cosmetics lady just waved me off. 'Come back towards Christmas.' Yeah, sure thing, if I haven't starved to death by then.

For twelve years my head's been crammed with useless stuff. I mean, do I seriously need to know about tectonic plates? Or the periodic table? And what the hell's the fascination with Shakespeare? If I wanted to study a foreign language I would've stuck with Japanese. And polynomials? I can barely remember what they are let alone what to do with them.

Every morning I wake up worrying about all the things I don't know. Like how to do a proper budget — not the baby budget we did in Year 11. How to change the oil in my car. What to do when the lights don't come back on after I've flicked the circuit breaker. How to fix the washing machine when the inlet valve light flashes red. How to act confident in a job interview without seeming stuck up. How to cook something that doesn't involve pasta. How to deal with the guys who hang out the car window making sucking noises at me. If I opened a school, I'd teach all those things, ya know, something useful. For life.

I can't talk to my parents about
any of this. They're still living
on Planet Delusion, ruled by me, "It
girl", ready to take on the world.
Yeah, I know, if I'm so popular then
why the hell don't I just talk to my
friends? Well, I would if they were
here but they're all in Europe right
now. Allegra's parents are rich so
they funded her entire trip. Tessa's
parents gave her five grand, saying
'You only turn eighteen once!' The
other girls saved up from their
crappy jobs the past few years.
Well, I didn't have time for a job
when I was at school cos being me
was a full-time job! Not that it's
gotten me anywhere.

Serious tone.

In closing, your Honour — isn't
that what I'm supposed to say?
I've watched a lot of Law & Order,
ya know. In closing, I'm suing my
school for false and misleading
behaviour. For not delivering the
reward they promised. I'm suing my
friends for using me to survive high
school, only to go off and enjoy life
without me. And I'm suing my parents
too. For leading me to believe every
crappy bit of artwork I did was
award winning, every song I sang was
'the voice of an angel'. For telling

me that 'the sky's the limit'. Well,
the sky's not the limit. Reality's
the limit. How would you feel if
you just found out your twelve-
year investment was a sham, if you
learned there's no security for the
futures you've been trading? That
the payoff for your backbreaking
work, for the stress and sleepless
nights, the sacrifices and second-
guessing is no job and a head full
of nothing?

Yeah, I'm still pretty. Pretty
fucking stupid.

Mood shift — upbeat. Checks phone/time.

Okay, this video is probably gonna
run way too long so I'll end it
here. Please subscribe to my
channel. And leave a comment below,
especially if you've had the same
experience. I reckon we've got a
good shot at a class action. See you
next week!

*****

SHE

Nicky buttons up their shirt, restrained.

She's pushy. Always challenging me
no matter what I do or say. I've
tried to ignore her. Easier said
than done when she's going at me
24/7. Worse, she's always wanting
me to hang out with the girls. If
she had her way, I'd be heading to
the mall for the perfect brows. Or
watching a silk dress glide over her
skin.

Every hair standing on high alert.
Every nerve cell tingling with a
sense of longing. A sweet, sweaty
jumble of confusion.

People sneer and scoff.
Or worse. A few weeks ago, I got
the shit beaten out of me after
school, just because I let her have
her way. Even with my face planted
on the ground, I could see Mason in
the distance. Watching. Then walking
away. I wore my bruises as a badge
of honour … of the line I drew in
the sand long ago to protect her, to
allow her true nature to flourish. To
let the whole world see that I was
proud to stand with her. Then the
tide came in, like it always does,

destroying everything in its wake.
Except the pain. It'll take more
than an ocean to crush that.

Just when I think I'm finally
starting to understand who she is,
and what she wants, she confuses
the hell out of me, always trying
to get me to do or say something
that I just know is gonna add to
the shit I'm already treading
through. But I trudge ahead anyway,
drawn to her, deeper and deeper. No
questions. No limits. Lately, she's
getting feisty, I mean really over
the top. Screaming at me, calling
me a fake. Saying I'm just some
uptight asshole like all the others,
too concerned about what everyone
else thinks. Like last night, when
she told me I was a shell, no guts
at all, no substance. 'You're the
fucking hollowman,' she hissed, 'you
disgust me!' and she was right.
I'm a shapeshifter, masquerading
as someone I'm not. When she was
done, I couldn't do or say anything.
I couldn't pull back my shoulders
and stand tall. My spine hunched
forward, each vertebra curving
instinctively to hide myself from
her.

Then this morning, when I was still
trying to process last night's

mood shift, she's oozing apologies,
beckoning me forward, the glint
in her eyes growing bigger and
brighter. Each word brought us
closer. I hadn't heard that kind
of excitement in her voice in ages
… the freedom, the release as she
kept calling it. How everything
would be so much easier. Better. Our
bodies as one. The desire explosive.
Unimaginable. Something in her
voice, in her eyes, was different.

Urgent. Like her survival depended
on what I did next. That's how I
knew the time had come. I've waited
my whole life, wondering if I'd
recognise the moment when it finally
arrived. All those close calls
flooded back, the sense of being so
near yet so far, the emptiness that
crept in each time I stepped to the
edge, too petrified to fling open
my arms and leap. To float outside
myself. But this time, I was being
pulled towards an energy so natural,
so right, that I finally felt ...
centred and I knew I wanted that
feeling all the time. I needed it.
To breathe it in, to feel alive.

I ran to Mum, telling her it was
time and she burst into tears,
big gulping sobs, screeching
'Nickyyyyyyyy!' Her hand was

reaching for me but I didn't take it. I couldn't take it. Because she was just trying to hold on to a piece of herself. To her past. She told me I was just confused, that there were people who could help me. I laughed because in that moment her desperation for 'a cure', as she kept calling it, suddenly struck me as funny. That she thinks I have some sort of mental illness because I don't fit into a box. 'If my head's fucked,' I told Mum, 'it's not because of WHO I am. It's because no one will let me BE who I am.' She collapsed to the floor, her legs folding in slow motion, crushed by the weight of truth.

Dad didn't say anything. He just stared at me, riveted to the spot by contempt. His eyes narrowed, small and dark like black pebbles, robbed of all emotion as though the fatherhood part of his heart had just detached. The man who had patted me firmly on the back when my tears came, unable — maybe just unwilling — to show emotion when I was bruised and defeated by him and all the people like him who expect me to be someone I'm not. We didn't move. Or speak. Our truths enveloped us, parallel curves unable to converge.

Then she screamed, a howl of
anguish ripping through me like a
shard of glass. Mum and Dad stood
united, their ears and minds closed,
oblivious to the deafening noise
coming from the woman standing
right in front of them. The woman
with a sparkle in her eyes, pulling
me towards her, crying that it
was time, that there was no other
choice, no other way for her to
survive. That she was my future.
That her body was my body. Its
curves. Its edges.

That she is me.

* * * * *

LIFELINE

Movement piece.

*Sound/music conveys discord and dissonance.
By the end of the piece, the beat has become
weaker and more erratic.*

*There is a sense that all of the characters
are struggling, searching for connection but
unable to reach out.*

ROLLER COASTER

Lexy shifts awkwardly, taking her time to speak.

I never liked roller coasters. My brother Robby used to drag me on the big one at Funland, this dodgy carnival that always sprung up around Christmas. We'd tear around the bends, strapped in a heap of metal, flying through the loop de loops, then climbing up, up, up, shitting ourselves before the final plunge.

When we walked off, still spinning, Mum'd shove coins in Robby's hand for another go like she needed a break from us that bad. Robby reckons she was half hoping we'd fly off the tracks so she could get her old life back. 'When I wasn't a friggin' maid, picking up your crap all the time… reading that shit book with the turtle who was so goddamn slow he never got anywhere. Just like yous two.'

Maybe that's why I loved all those sappy TV movies around Christmas. You know the ones I'm talking about … where the kids always got brand

new toys, and the family would sit
around a massive table with the
perfect golden-brown turkey in the
centre. All the cousins would be
there, singing Christmas carols, and
everyone knew all the words. Someone
would have learned an old-fashioned
lesson and everyone'd be smiling,
or hugging, or holding hands. Then
after dinner they'd head outside
and make angels in the snow, or the
world's best snowman with a carrot
nose and a little pipe.

Sarcastically.

Dontcha love happy endings? I don't.
There was no coal in our house on
Christmas morning, but there were
no presents either. Mum was usually
passed out on the sofa with an empty
bottle nearby, sometimes two. One
year I found her on the floor covered
in vomit. Uncle Pete said she was
lucky she didn't choke and die. And
I've never told anyone this before
but … sometimes I wish she did. So
I could get off the roller coaster.
So I could live somewhere else. Cos
anywhere's better than home.

When I was little, television was
my escape. All the families were
so supportive, so … nice. It didn't
take me long to see mine came up

short. But then I got older and
worked out that the TV families were
bullshit, that this was the real
world and I better get used to it.
All my friends were always whinging
about their families and their
houses and all the stuff they didn't
have, so I figured their lives sucked
as much as mine. But the more I
got to know them, to hang out where
they lived and meet their parents,
and brothers and sisters, sometimes
even their grandparents, I could see
their lives were just like the ones
on TV, in full colour. Most of them
had a mum and dad at home, and even
the parents who split up were still
talking to each other. My life's in
black and white. I've never even
met my dad. Mum said he didn't want
anything to do with her, or Robby
and me, and 'There's not a goddamn
thing we can do about it!'

My friend Freya's always saying her
mother's such a bitch but I reckon
she's the bitch, always telling her
Mum to fuck off whenever she asks
about school, or about anything
really. Like yesterday, when Freya
got all worked up, shouting and
crying, then storming out of the
kitchen. Her mum turned to me and
smiled, but it was an awkward smile
like she couldn't move her lips

properly, and she asked, 'Lexy, do you talk to your mother like that?' I laughed, even though it wasn't really funny, cos my mother'd kill me if I talked to her like Freya, then I told her, 'Mum never asks about school … or anything really.' Her eyebrows went up and her sigh was so deep I could feel her breath. I explained Mum's not around much, and when she's around, she's not really there anyway. Her eyes were watery so I passed her a tissue and said, 'Don't worry, I'm seventeen. I can look after myself!' but she just shook her head. Then she patted my hand and said how brave I was to share all that. And the minute she said 'brave' something funny happened. My bottom lip started quivering and suddenly I didn't feel real brave at all. Then my mouth opened and the words flew out too fast to catch them. I told her all the stuff that's bubbling up inside me, all the feelings about how I'm not good enough and Mum would be happier without me. How Dad doesn't even wanna know me. How Mason's gotten all intense lately, not saying much and taking forever to answer my texts, then when he finally does, he just talks shit like he doesn't even wanna be with me. I told her I feel like I'm a piece, a fragment that's missing all the good bits but I don't

know where to find the rest … the
parts I need to work properly. I bet
they wouldn't fit anyway.

When I finally stopped talking,
Freya's mum said nothing. She
just stared at me, and smack in
the centre of her eyes, I saw my
reflection. Except it didn't really
look like me, and I wondered if
that's how everyone sees me. She
reached across the table and
squeezed my hand, gently at first
then real tight, like she needed to
hold on. She told me I could talk to
her anytime but there are people I
can talk to who are professionals,
who are trained to help deal
with everything I'm feeling. Then
she tore off a sheet of paper and
scribbled a name and a phone number.

And that's why I'm here.

* * * * *

NOW YOU SEE ME

Mason struggles to rise as though an unseen weight is pushing him down.

Last night when I showed my father my ATAR estimate, I thought he'd crack open the champagne. But instead his mouth formed a straight line, all cos I'm a point off the max. 'I didn't raise you to come second best.' Then he shoved the slip in my hand, said it's crunch time and I better hit the books. What does he think I've been doing for the past twelve years? Now Lexy's hassling me when I don't reply within thirty seconds, carrying on about how she just has to get out of the house and why don't I take her somewhere? She's so insecure, ever since that photo was Snapchatted all over school last week… the one of my abs that little sneak took when I whipped off my shirt after training. Reena, I think that's her name. Girls get the shits when guys give them a number and yeah, it's not real enlightened of us to say someone's a '9' or a '6.5 at best'. But that doesn't stop them from shouting, 'Mason, show us your abs!' Girls are always going on about how they're limited by

society. By men. But we're typecast
too. Men drive trucks, men play
sport. Men swear, men roar. Men are
strong. Men don't cry. Men don't ask
for help.

Phone buzzes, reads message.

This just in from Lexy, the drama
queen … 'I can't do this anymore
Mace. You're so self-absorbed, you
can't make room for anyone else.'

Tosses phone.

I used to be able to pretend that
everything was okay. I'd tell myself
I was just having a crap day, that
things could only get better. But
I'm not as strong as you think. The
darkness crept up on me over months,
years, like a bad headache. The kind
you think will pass if just take
your mind off it for a while. But
it never went away. It got worse.
Much worse. Last year I saw a school
counsellor and that helped. For a
while. He was always going on about
resilience, telling me life's full
of ups and downs. As if I didn't
already know. But resilience feeds
off freedom. How can I recover, how
can I bounce back, when everyone's
scripting my life? When everyone
wants a piece of me? When every day

is an effort, an endless horizon of
deadlines, expectations and false
promises?

Imitates speakers.

'Hurry, you'll be late for work!'
'Have you studied for your exams?'
'Did you put petrol in the car?'
'Mason, we need you to give a speech
at the assembly on Friday.' 'Mace,
we never go out anymore!' And the
biggest lie of all: 'When you're
an adult you can do what you want.'
That's bullshit. I turned eighteen
last month and nothing's changed.
Nothing!

I've sacrificed heaps to make Dad
proud. Given up things I want to do,
spent time doing things I don't want
to do. And ya know what's strange?
I'm so used it now I can't even work
out which is which anymore. Every
day I wake up, it's the same shit
all over again. And why? So I can
get into the best uni and land a top
job? So I can work my ass off making
money to buy things I don't need? So
I can take on more responsibilities
that'll keep me so busy, so
stressed, that I won't even know my
own family? Like him.

Silence.

You used to say, 'Deep breath, don't give up, honey. Everything will be okay.' But you're not here anymore, are you?

Emotion building.

I can hardly remember your voice.

Pause.

How could you give up so easily?

Shift of energy/focus.

Our whole school photo came out today. That's me front and centre with my leadership smile switched on, surrounded by nearly fifteen hundred beaming faces … and I never felt so lonely. And useless.

Pause.

I'm a fraud. Nicky was getting beaten up and what did I do? I walked away. I'm oblivious. We're all oblivious. Scratch the surface but there's no solid core … it's veneer all the way through. We're drifters. Moving all the time, too busy to look beyond ourselves. Can anyone put down their fucking phone and really see me? Maybe they're

too afraid to be still, cos maybe
then they'll have time to think,
and they'll realise how meaningless
their lives are too.

They call it the black dog. But
it's not a dog. A dog can be cute,
cuddly. Loyal. A dog can help you
find your way home when you lose
direction. When there's no clear
path. This is a wolf. A savage beast
that attacks, sinking its teeth
in. That tears off flesh to get to
the insides, leaving mangled bones.
I'm a black hole, a star that's
collapsed in on itself, sucking
in all the light. I've been tired
for so long that I don't remember
what it's like to feel good. To
be normal. To sleep when you're
supposed to and to wake up, looking
forward to the day. To the things
you'll be doing. The people you'll
be seeing. To your future.

Lies down, becoming smaller.

Problem is you get used to the
darkness. The lumpy weight moulds
to your shape, like a well-worn coat
that you can't possibly take off
because it's cold. It's so cold.

Losing energy.

> And heavy.

Breathing deep and slow.

> I can't breathe.

Beat.

> Is that how you felt? That everything was too hard?

Laboured breathing.

> Or were you just tired of hurting?

Pause.

> I'm tired of hurting, too.

*****

FATAL ERROR (Coding)

Tightly choreographed. Narration pre-recorded by a single voice. All character lines spoken.

MASON stands tentatively on a precipice, unseen by characters. Remaining cast moves in perfect syncronisation, adopting strong, precise gestures and severe movements as the piece transitions from functionality to malfunction to agency.

NARRATION

Coding is getting the computer.
To see what you see.
It's easy, just talk to it.
But don't use words.
Computers can't understand them.
Only on and off switches.
Ones and zeros.
   Are you a one?
   Or a zero?

Coding is power. And choice.
You can write any script you like.
Lines and lines of codes that you put into a program.
An exe file.
So anyone can use it.

Coding is telling the computer how to do something. How to change what's in its memory.

I want to change my memory.
But I don't know how.

Coding is a language.
Make sure you know the lingo.

Function.
Content.
Instructions.

Script.
Compile.
Exceptions.

Thread.
Loop.
Run time.

Scratch.
Glitch.
Fragments.

Submit.
Test.
Escape.

Anyone can write a code.

LEXY
Code Lexy. Happy endings.

MILA
Code Mila. Popularity.

VIJAY
Code Vijay. Belonging.

WILL
Code Will. Acceptance.

NICKY
Code Nicky. Truth.

FREYA
Code Freya. Fearless.

REENA
Code Reena. Perfection.

LEXY searches for MASON. Checks phone, confused.
LEXY
Has anyone seen Mason?

A storm gathers. Actors form shadowed clusters, moving haphazardly as soundscape of computer malfunction/alarm builds. LEXY weaves in and out of cast, searching for MASON.

NARRATION
Coders make mistakes.
Bugs.
Errors.
Flaws.

Computer malfunction soundscape peaks in volume/intensity.

> **LEXY**
> Maaaaaaaaa-son?

> **NARRATION**
> Failures.
> Faults.

Malfunction soundscape out.

> The first step of coding is to
> realise there's more than one way to
> solve a problem.

*New cast clusters form as others realise
MASON is missing and search with urgency.*

> Sometimes, it just takes a while.
> For someone to find you.

> You need time and space to think.

> **LEXY**
LEXY searches frantically for MASON.

> Mason?

> **NARRATION**
> Or not think.

> To test.
>   To rest.
> To be.
>   To not be.
> To go.

LEXY sees MASON.

LEXY
Mason!

NARRATION
To stay.

Mason's stance becomes steady. Sound of computer rebooting.

ALL
And try again.

HERE AND NOW (Epilogue)

This transition bookends Fight Song, using the same design elements of disconnection to reach a place of connectedness. This is not the private world or public world of each character. It is a new more "real" world where each character is moving towards their true self, tentatively but with a sense of authenticity and awareness of others.

ALL
In our skin, we're here.
Fighting.
Still fighting.

LEXY
For your time.

WILL
For your heart.

VIJAY
For your friendship.

NICKY
For a chance.

FREYA
For a smile.

REENA
For attention.

                    MILA
        For love.

                    MASON
        For hope.

Lights out.

STUDY GUIDE

STUDY GUIDE

Maura Pierlot © 2020

Eight young people navigating high school and beyond, each struggling to hold on – to family, to friends, to a piece of themselves.

FRAGMENTS

fragmentstheplay.com

Photo: Novel Photographic, courtesy of The Street Theatre

FRAGMENTS DEBUT SEASON
SOLD OUT

Photo: Jessica Conway, courtesy of The Street Theatre

DURATION:
Fragments is approximately 85-minutes duration *(no interval)*.

AUDIENCE:
Suitable for Years 9-12, with modified activities offered for younger students (Years 7-8).

Please note: *Fragments* contains strong language and themes.

λ

TABLE OF CONTENTS

Photo: Creswick Collective,
courtesy of The Street Theatre

How to Use These Notes

This study guide is intended to be used in the classroom to explore issues and themes featured in *Fragments*, and to support and extend students' knowledge and understanding of the work, whether through reading, dissecting, analysing or performing the text. Students are encouraged to explore the many issues and themes highlighted in the work, and the potential of drama/theatre to cast a light on contemporary issues in society. They are also encouraged to explore context and perspective by reading the statements from the playwright and director at the start of this publication, particularly their intentions for the work.

Fragments has good cross-disciplinary relevance (The Arts, English, HPE, Civics and Citizenship), as outlined under Australian Curriculum on pages 5-8. However, this document is intended as a guide only, and teachers and students are encouraged to introduce their own ideas and experiences in the classroom. The playwright thanks you for choosing her work and welcomes your feedback via email: maura@maurapierlot.com.

WHAT IS *FRAGMENTS* ABOUT?

Eight young people navigating high school and beyond, each struggling to hold on – to family, to friends, to a piece of themselves.

Perhaps you know them. The bubbly girl who keeps telling you she's okay. The high achiever who's suddenly so intense. The young teen obsessed with social media. The boy challenged by communication. Every single day they, and others, are working hard to keep it together. So hard, they don't see their friends are struggling, too.

Through eight imagined stories, *Fragments* moves from a place of disconnection to connectedness.

The action of *Fragments* takes place in the minds and hearts of an ordinary group of eight young people. Although set in Australia, their stories could take place anywhere.

THEMES

Anxiety, Depression, Neurodivergence, Academic success, Peer pressure, Isolation, Self-identity, Family dysfunction, Bullying, Gender dysphoria, Eating disorders, Heritage and cultural identity, Body dysmorphia, Relationships, Suicide.

CHARACTERS

All of the characters currently attend the same school, except Mila who has graduated and is in her gap year.

WILL	16-year-old male	**FREYA**	15-year-old female
VIJAY	14-year-old male	**REENA**	13-year-old female
MILA	18-year-old female	**NICKY**	17-year-old trans female presenting as male
LEXY	17-year-old female	**MASON**	18-year-old male

MONOLOGUE SYNOPSES

Short Circuit

Drawn to rhythm, Will struggles in a world of words, unable to connect to the girl of his dreams, but refusing medication that will make him think like everyone else.

In My Head

On the outside Freya's a normal teen but on the inside, she's fighting anxiety every single day, alone and unable to tell anyone that she needs help.

Good for Nothing

Worried he'll never be tall enough, handsome enough or smart enough, Vijay turns to social media to chat up girls at school, with devastating consequences.

Picture Perfect

Convinced she's fat, Reena relies on filters to market a better version of herself online, revelling in praise from a growing legion of followers.

Pretty Stupid

Reeling from an abrupt reality check, Mila sues her school and family for failing to prepare her for life after graduation.

She

Every day Nicky fights to be heard, to dress as she wants, to be who she is ... until one day when she must make a choice, knowing she can never be free as long as he lives.

Roller Coaster

Lexy is determined to internalise her family struggles until a chance meeting opens the floodgates and changes the course of her life.

Now You See Me

Everyone's so busy looking up to Mason that they don't recognise the debilitating depression that is taking over his life.

Australian Curriculum

ENGLISH

STRAND	CONTENT DESCRIPTION	YEAR 9	YEAR 10
Language	Language for interaction	ACELA 1551	ACELA 1564
Literature	Responding to literature	ACELT 1771 ACELT 1634 ACELT 1635	ACELT 1640 ACELT 1641
	Examining literature	ACELT 1636 ACELT 1637 ACELT 1772	ACELT 1774
	Creating literature	ACELT 1773	ACELT 1814
Literacy	Texts in context	ACELY 1739	ACELY 1749
	Interacting with others	ACELY 1740 ACELY 1811 ACELY 1741	ACELY 1750 ACELY 1813 ACELY 1751
	Interpreting, analysing, evaluting	ACELY 1744	
	Creating texts	ACELY 1746	ACELY 1756

THE ARTS

STRAND	CONTENT DESCRIPTION	YEAR 9	YEAR 10
Drama	Improvise with the elements of drama and narrative structure	ACADRM047	
	Manipulate combinations of the elements of drama to develop and convey the physical and psychological aspects of roles and characters	ACADRM048	
	Practise and refine the expressive capacity of voice and movement to communicate ideas	ACADRM049	
	Perform devised and scripted drama making deliberate artistic elements to unify dramatic meaning for an audience	ACADRM051	
Music	Plan and organise compositions with an understanding of style and convention, including drawing upon Australian music by Aboriginal and Torres Strait Islander artists	ACAMUM102	

THE ARTS cont.

STRAND	CONTENT DESCRIPTION	YEAR 9	YEAR 10
Media Arts	Manipulate media representations to identify and examine social and cultural values and beliefs, including those of Aboriginal and Torres Strait Islander Peoples	ACADAM074	
Visual Arts	Manipulate materials, techniques, technologies and processes to develop and represent their own artistic intentions	ACADAM126	
Dance	Manipulate combinations of the elements of dance and choreographic devices to communicate their choreographic intent	ACADAM021	

HEALTH & PE

STRAND	CONTENT DESCRIPTION	YEAR 9	YEAR 10
Personal, Social & Community Health	Communicating and interacting for health and wellbeing	ACPPS094	

CIVICS & CITIZENSHIPS

STRAND	CONTENT DESCRIPTION	YEAR 9	YEAR 10
Knowledge & Understanding	Citizenship, diversity and identity	ACHCK080	
Skills	Analysis, synthesis and interpretation	ACHCS084 ACHCS085	ACHCS098
	Problem-solving and decision-making	ACHCS086	ACHCS099

Notes on the following activities:

- All activities have been designed for students in Years 9 and 10 to align with curriculum outcomes.

- Where relevant, adjustments have been suggested for Years 7-8, and Years 11-12. The adjustments are designed as stimulus, rather than complete activities and while not directly linked, are relevant to curriculum outcomes for this age range.

- Drama is the primary focus from The Arts; however, other strands are also relevant and list ideas to get teachers started, rather than comprising a full unit of work.

ACTIVITIES - *Before* reading the play

LEARNING AREA - ENGLISH

ACTIVITY YEARS 9 - 10	ADJUSTMENTS
Tap into prior knowledge and social context • Discuss the title of the play - *Fragments*. What could it be about? What is a fragment? How can the word be used? • Read the *Interview with the Playwright* and *From the Director* - what do you think the play is about now? • How is mental illness perceived in Australian Society today? In the past? What about the future? What are the main challenges faced by young people today? • In groups, or as a whole class begin the creation of a Lotus Diagram Resource 1 Identify up to eight subtopics under the main heading of 'Youth Mental Health'. • Read and discuss each monologue synopsis. What is the main issue addressed in each monologue? What do you think it will be about? Where does it fit on the Lotus Diagram?	**Years 7 - 8** Many issues raised in *Fragments* are also addressed in the Years 7-8 Health curriculum. A modified Lotus Diagram, or a simpler Cluster Diagram[Resource 1] may be used. **Years 11-12** Students in Years 11 and 12 may be able to work more independently on the given activities or may wish to explore them further. Creation of a personal reading list could be worthwhile pursuing, and a more detailed text analysis and comparison.

- Brainstorm and start collecting a list of media and texts that address youth mental health issues and challenges. These may include novels, short stories, blog posts, dramatic performances, movies, songs or artworks.

Resource 1: Lotus Diagram / Cluster Diagram
https://creately.com./blog/diagrams/types-of-graphic-organizers/#Brainstorming

LEARNING AREA - THE ARTS: DRAMA

Role Play

- Form small groups of 4-6 students and ask the groups to select an issue/theme relevant to *Fragments*, e.g. bullying, social media, anxiety, depression, neurodivergence.

- Allocate a student to be the person experiencing the issue (change roles often).

Years 7 - 8

Drama students in Years 7 and 8 may do a modified version of this activity.

- Present possible real-life scenarios and have each student act as themselves in the scenario.

- Allow students to make decisions and challenge them. This could be through changing the scenario (e.g. adding a character, changing the setting, changing the response).

- Ask the students to reflect on their actions:
  - What could they have done better?
  - Why did they react the way they did?
  - Is there anyone to blame for their actions?
  - Who was the instigator?

LEARNING AREA - HEALTH & PE

Looking after friends

Ask students to discuss what would they do if they believed a friend was experiencing stress?

- How would you approach your friend?

- What would you say to them?

Years 7 - 8
Discuss the importance of valuing diversity and the strategies for demonstrating empathy and sensitivity.

LEARNING AREA - CIVICS & CITIZENSHIP

Influence of media and social media

- Briefly discuss the central themes of *Fragments* as a whole, and of each monologue.

Years 7 - 8
Focusing on a selection of themes from *Fragments*, discuss different perspectives and the language used around these.

ACTIVITIES - *During/After* reading the play

LEARNING AREA - ENGLISH

FOCUS AREA	ACTIVITY YEARS 9 - 10	ADJUSTMENTS
Initial Response	Which monologue/character do you identify most with and why? Write your own short monologue in your voice, or that of a fictitious character, responding to what you have read and how it makes you feel. Keep a list of the key themes, challenges and issues as they arise. Do they overlap? Are there any common themes? Are the issues and challenges faced by the characters in *Fragments* universal? Do/will they transcend time? Discuss.	**Years 7-8** Activities listed for Years 9-10 may be modified to meet outcomes for Years 7-8, noting modification of some themes may be necessary. **Initial response** Focus on a smaller selection of themes, discussing and exploring those that are immediately relevant to the students' world.
Close Study	Critique one of the monologues, focusing on plot, pacing and stylistic conventions. Is the character (and their language) credible? What literary techniques does the playwright use? Does the monologue reach a satisfying conclusion?	**Close study** Focus on language use to meet specific purposes, e.g. character development, influencing opinion.

Consider the language used throughout the play. What does it reveal about the characters? How does it make the reader feel?

Ask students to select a short scene from their lives and try to emulate the playwright's style in a monologue.

What role do the post-dramatic transitions serve in storytelling? Would the monologues have the same impact if performed alone rather than as part of a unified work? Why do you think the playwright used this technique?

Close Study cont.

As a class, in groups or individually, students compose an email to the playwright. In this they should identify the impact the play has had on them. Which parts resonated? Which ones didn't? How did they feel about the themes? The style? How do they feel about an adult writing the voice of today's youth? Do they see a sequel as viable and, if so, how could this be done? As a novel? A play? A series of short stories? What issues are there still to be covered?

| **Significance** | Compare and contrast a *Fragments* monologue to another text, e.g. Vijay ('Good for Nothing') and *The Perks of Being a Wallflower* (book/film); Lexy ('Rollercoaster') and *Euphoria* (TV show).

Complete a chart, comparing and contrasting: theme, central characters, ending, setting, personal response.

In the 'Fatal Error (Coding)' scene, the narrator says:

Coding is power. And choice. You can write any script you like.

The scene acts as a turning point for the characters, particularly Mason. Discuss the concept of 'coding' and how it is relevant to the characters, and to the youth of today. Write a response to this from the point of view of one of the characters, maintaining their voice and attitudes. | **Significance** Compare and contrast characters within *Fragments*. |
|---|---|---|
| **Informed Reaction** | Write a character backstory or diary blog as the character, using prompts from the script:

• I've never been good with words. (Will);

• Fat! Fat! FAT! (Reena). | **Informed reaction** Experiment with language features to create new, short paragraphs/texts. |

| | Design a cover or promotional poster for *Fragments* and write a 100-word blurb to go with it. |
| **Informed Reaction cont.** | Write a short story, or new monologue about the same event but from a different perspective, e.g. What if Vijay were a female character? What if Nicky lived in a different country, or time period? |

Years 11-12

Activities for Years 9-10 may be modified and extended to meet outcomes in:

Essential English

Unit 3

- Points of view
- Perspectives
- Values

Unit 4

- Global, local and community issues
- Language choice

English

Unit 4

- Challenge perspectives, values and attitudes
- Relationship between voice and perspective

Literature

Unit 4

- Structural and stylistic features of plays
- Representation of values and ideas

LEARNING AREA - ENGLISH & DRAMA

FOCUS AREA	ACTIVITY YEARS 9 - 10	ADJUSTMENTS
Creative Response	Any of these activities are suitable for both English and Drama: • Write a monologue from another character's perspective. • Write a monologue from the perspective of the character's public self vs private self. • Discuss who the character is addressing (e.g. themselves, a peer, parent, psychologist)? • Choose a different audience for the character and discuss how the language, tone and energy of the text/performance changes. • Work in character pairs (e.g. Vijay and Reena, Freya and Will) to write new material from other character's perspective.	**Years 7-8** Similar activities may be undertaken. **Years 11-12** Write new material, or the next scene (epilogue), or a prologue, keeping the style consistent.

LEARNING AREA - THE ARTS: DRAMA
(Developed in consultation with Shelly Higgs)

FOCUS AREA	ACTIVITY YEARS 9 - 10	ADJUSTMENTS
Interpretive	**Individual:** Choose a character and devise a movement piece as a free-flowing and improvisational exercise that charts their emotional journey throughout their monologue. No words. Focus on rhythm and pace, use different levels and space. Does your character move quickly or slowly, and how do they change from beginning to end? What unseen pressures are on them (e.g. Mason)? **Group:** Choose a character and improvise a movement piece around (and with) the other characters. Do you go towards people or away from them? How does the presence of someone else effect your own movement? Focus on rhythm and pace, ebb and flow and use of different levels and space. This exercise is all about response so be aware of how you are affected by others and how you affect them.	**Years 7-8** Drama students in Years 7 and 8 may do a modified version of some or all of the listed activities. They will explore and experiment with voice, roles and dramatic techniques as guided by the teacher. They may work with modified scripts, or through improvisation.

Talk	In groups of 3+ students: Students form a circle with their backs turned to a student, who stands inside the circle as a character from the play. Students start talking judgmentally about the character in the middle of the circle. As the character, try to get the people in the circle to turn around and face you by responding to them, explaining yourself. How successful are you? Do you even want to try? What does this say about your character's self-esteem? Now switch roles - make sure everyone experiences what it's like to be the character in the middle of the circle.
Walk / Gesture	**Walk:** Walk as yourself, then walk in the shoes of your chosen character. Adopt mannerisms, facial expressions and interactions in character. How fast does your character walk? What part of their body leads? How visible do they want to be? Change your pace, posture, presenting part and see how this changes your character (e.g. shoulders back and chest forward vs hunched over and small).

Walk / Gesture cont.	**Gesture:** Come up with a gesture for your character (wringing hands, tapping leg, shrugging etc.). Amplify this gesture from "1" (being a normal gesture we wouldn't notice) to "10", where the gesture takes over the entire movement of the character. What does this tell you about your character?

Place yourself in different scenarios (e.g. school, home, activities) What changes? What stays the same? What triggers the character in different scenarios? |
| **Fear** | Identify the main fears for each of the characters or for your character of your choice.

Is fear blocking them from an action or emotion?

What would happen in the absence of fear? (For example, if Reena was interested in, and pursuing, Vijay?) |
| **Create** | Physically move around the space to create a world that exists in the chosen character's head. Allow yourself to be as abstract as possible (be open to any movement, ideas, words). This is a great exercise for character development and performance, allowing the actor to be fully present without relying on words. |

Physical/ Somatic	Try overexaggerating the script and words. For example: Freya struggles with anxiety. If you haven't experienced anxiety before, what do you think it would feel like? How would a person speak when trying to describe anxiety to another?
	Try reading/performing In My Head (Freya's monologue) as though you cannot catch your breath. Note how that affects your emotions and performance. Try the same with others experiencing breathlessness around you. Try reading/performing Now You See Me (Mason's monologue) as someone not able to move, i.e., being held down or pulled back by others. Or try reading/performing Short Circuit (Will's monologue) with emphasis on rhythm/tapping.
Pressure Test	Put the characters under pressure from peers.
	• What would make the characters do something they didn't want to do?
	• What would it take for them to not give in to their peers?

Imagery	Explore imagery in one or more monologues. For example: In 'Picture Perfect' (Reena's monologue) explore the photocopier, mirror, self-portrait. • What does the imagery tell you about the characters, their self-image and their view of the world?	
Produce & Perform	Collaborate as a member of a drama production team to interpret, rehearse and perform *Fragments*.	

LEARNING AREA - THE ARTS: DANCE

FOCUS AREA	ACTIVITY YEARS 9 - 10	ADJUSTMENTS
Improv.	Take one element of *Fragments* – a theme, a character, an emotion – and choreograph a short dance sequence to portray the central message. Analyse and appraise your selections, including manipulation of elements.	**Years 7-8** Experiment with dance elements, select and perform a short sequence to convey a central emotion from *Fragments*.

LEARNING AREA - THE ARTS: VISUAL ARTS

FOCUS AREA	ACTIVITY YEARS 9 - 10	ADJUSTMENTS
Technique & Intention	Students select the monologue that resonates the most. Explore why this is? Is there empathy for the central character? Is there a connection? Experiment with different techniques and processes to produce a series of works expressing the emotions or central themes of the chosen monologue. Complete a rationale analysing the choices made and their impact on the overall artwork.	**Years 7-8** Explore symbols in different artworks, specifically those that reflect issues important to youth. Students design and incorporate their own symbol into an artwork based on a chosen element of *Fragments*.

LEARNING AREA - THE ARTS: MUSIC

FOCUS AREA	ACTIVITY YEARS 9 - 10	ADJUSTMENTS
Compose & Arrange	Students select a monologue that resonates with them. Explore the changing and evolving emotion associated with the monologue. Identify suitable styles or genres that could accompany the monologue. Using technology as a composition tool, or other sources, compose accompanying music to be played in the background of an excerpt of the spoken monologue.	**Years 7-8** Select a known piece of music and manipulate some elements to change the style, enhancing the connection with one of the themes in *Fragments*.

LEARNING AREA - THE ARTS: MEDIA ARTS

FOCUS AREA	ACTIVITY YEARS 9 - 10	ADJUSTMENTS
Re-imagining	As a group, list the key issues in youth mental health and wellbeing that are raised throughout *Fragments*. Explore and identify where these are represented in the media. Locate multiple viewpoints if possible. Select from a range of images, soundbites and artworks, including those produced by the student, and remix these to produce a new version that presents a variety of viewpoints.	**Years 7-8** Create a media artwork to represent a key theme in *Fragments*, using a combination of technical and symbolic elements.

LEARNING AREA - HEALTH & PE

FOCUS AREA	ACTIVITY YEARS 9 - 10	ADJUSTMENTS
Communicating & Interacting for Health / Wellbeing	After reading the play, revisit the questions asked in the pre-reading activity. Discuss any changes in perspectives and attitudes. Select one of the characters and create a strategy or an action plan to assist and support this character. The plan may be presented as a flow chart, brochure, fact sheet, role-play script or in a form of the student's choice.	**Years 7-8** Revisit discussion from pre-reading activity. Generate a list of actions to support the mental health and wellbeing of others.

LEARNING AREA - CIVICS & CITIZENSHIP

FOCUS AREA	ACTIVITY YEARS 9 - 10	ADJUSTMENTS
Communicating & Interacting for Health / Wellbeing cont.	Select a challenge experienced by one of the characters in *Fragments*. Critically analyse the points raised in the monologue in relation to stereotypes, assumptions, bias and impact. Further explore the mental health issue through media and other sources. Identify trends and change over time. Devise and present evidence-based strategies for negotiation and conflict resolution that considers multiple perspectives and, if applicable, the legal system.	**Years 7-8** Focusing on one of the monologues, identify different perspectives and what may have informed them. Recognise assumptions that are made and suggest inclusive practices as mediation strategies.

(With the exception of Drama, all activities and curriculum links were developed in consultation with Kellie Nissen, Just Right Words.)

FRAGMENTS REVIEWS

New Territory
https://www.actwriters.org/new-territory-blog/fragments

Canberra Critics Circle
http://bit.ly/FragmentsReviewCCC

ArtsHub
http://bit.ly/FragmentsArtsHubReview

RESOURCES (mental health)

Early intervention, support and treatment key to managing mental health conditions in young people
http://bit.ly/HealthyFamiliesBeyondBlue

Increased rates of anxiety and depression reported during COVID-19
https://www.livescience.com/depression-anxiety-increase-covid-19.html

Social isolation and loneliness can be harmful to both mental and physical health
http://bit.ly/AIHWSocialIsolation

Wellbeing during times of uncertainty
http://bit.ly/GoodGriefSelfCare

Youth mental health issues on the rise during COVID-19
http://bit.ly/YouthMentalHealthCrisis

CPSIA information can be obtained
at www.ICGtesting.com
Printed in the USA
LVHW052045100921
697564LV00003B/300